CAIRN CITY

By John Elkin

This book is a work of fiction. Names, characters, organizations, places, events, and incidents either are the product of the author's imagination or are used fictitiously. Any resemblance to actual persons, living or dead, or actual events is coincidental.

INVOCATION

Muse! Guide my hands. I cannot resist. Describe to me places.
And I'll make them exist.

CONTENTS

A NOTE ON TOWNS..1

TALES..2
"Birds"..3
"The Adventurer"..4
"The Totem Hut"..5
"Half Out of Sight"..6
"How did we get here?"..7
"Worst Case Scenario"..8
"Ashlands"..9
"Syzygy"..10
"Desire Path"..11

~~~

WHISPERS..12

~~~

SLAM..19
"Perfect Words"..20
"White Flowers"..22
"Blockchain YHWH"..23
"Twin Tricks"..24
"Copper Island"..25
"Dolphins"..26
"Beginnings"..28
"Anubis"..29
"A Moment of Silence"..30

A NOTE ON MYSTERIES AND BEAVERS..........31

CLASSICAL..32
"Cultural Anthropology"..33
"Savior"..34
"The Portal"..35
"First Turnout"..37

"The Golden Horn"....................................38
"The Battle of Bull Run"............................39
"Camping in the Basement".......................40
"Undeniable"..42
"Chuck Heston"...43
"Gold Miners"...44
"Artificial Moons".......................................45
"Arts District"...46
"Mist on the Sacramento River"..................47
"William Blake"...48
"The Arrow"..49
"Ganymede"..50
"Fine Place To Fall In Love".......................51
"The Bachelor"..52
"Land of Knives"...53

A NOTE ON STONES AND POEMS.........54

A NOTE ON TOWNS

Many towns will be mentioned in this book. Some of these towns once existed. Some of them you could live next to or even be a resident. And yet some of them are of pure imagination. My poetic intention is for this book to serve as a sort of travel guide through places yes, but also people, experiences and particularly emotions.

I want you, by the end of this, to feel like a well journeyed traveller. Try to take an extra moment with each page, to close your eyes and manifest yourself within these towns. Say "Hello" to its people, speak out loud in their dialects, walk in their streets and trails, eat at their restaurants, take a part in their unique festivities. In essence, for that moment, to live there.

Some towns are quite happy towns, some towns could be unappealing. But all of them are worth a visit. A good town, like a good poem, is one which can be taken anywhere with you long after you leave it.

TALES

"Birds"

When the room grew lively and the rigid bravado of introduction had waned, the conversation turned to the subject of birds. And in this indirect way, which is the wont of men, each one shared who he was by the birds he grew up seeing:

--

Where I'm from birds as an animal had no name, but were identified by the noises each one made. There were those that made sounds like 'who who who' and others that made sounds like 'squawk squawk!' and more others like 'wrrrrrrrr'. And it was great fun to imitate their singing.

--

Where I'm from the men hunted the birds and dined on their meat. They were fearful of men and all people. Even children, who innocently reached to pet the beasts to know what one felt to touch, were narrowly rebuffed. We only knew how a dead bird felt.

--

Where I'm from the birds were huge. Wingtip to wingtip, and I'm not lying, was the size of a barn. Snatched up whole cattle and flew 'em to who knows where. Never took a person though. Old folks say back in mythological times our ancestors and the birds made a peace covenant which protected us.

--

Where I'm from the birds could tell the future. We had a religion of bird watching. What bird showed when and how many? What was the weather like when they showed? When you saw a bird it wasn't just some bird. It was the language of the gods speaking to you.

--

Where I'm from the birds have never flown. (And in those words the entire group grew quiet and uneasy again as it was when they first had gathered; for they all understood the implications of his words and felt pity. They knew he was born here. And has never felt that beatific flutter.)

"The Adventurer"

The adventurer spoke on the differences of things up close and at a distance. He talked of how miles tends to soften things. Gives 'em a painterly quality that flattens them into the backdrop of the landscape. Furry fuzzy looking hillsides ain't but prickly chaparral. The glistening ocean only a choppy drowning rage of water. The glowing godly planets just rocky lifeless balls of ice.

"Is it worth it to visit up close?" I asked. "Would it pain me so to know the truth? Would I ever enjoy a view again?"

The traveller, he tilted back his greasy battered cowboy hat to reveal a heavy lined sun-dried visage--eyes Sinbad blue. Before he left he said one thing that's made a lasting impression:
“One day that truth will meet you, regardless of you looking.”

"The Totem Hut"

Outcroppings of coal, by her childhood home. She once thought they could lead to mines of wealth for someone enterprising enough to excavate them. The ducks who she loves so much to visit. She fears she has not seen them enough for the playful names she gave them to live in her memory.

The children at the bridge hang their gloves and their phones carelessly over the railing. As if instead of a river flowing it was an air cushion below them. People wait in their parked cars. Engines running. Smoke coughing from the exhaust. But not moving. Perhaps they want to drive somewhere, but don't know where to go and sit frozen in indecision.

She makes her way by the aged tracks which cut a striped path through town. People walk their dogs by it, unafraid of trains by now. At night, she breaks the lock on the totem hut in the north end of the park. As a girl she'd always wondered what was in there. Nothing but brooms, a shovel and a stack of chairs it turns out. On the plane the next day one of the names of the ducks comes to her. She debates the idea writing it down somewhere. But what a silly thing to hold onto.

"Half out of Sight"

There is a thing out there.
Perhaps which connects all things.
Perhaps which can never be found or understood.
Perhaps we've always had it. Or it is ever out of our reach.

And all fine institutions are after this thing:
Philosophers, scientists, artists, theologians.
They don't know what this thing is, but they search.
They think they know where to look.

The sunset is just a sunset.
And she is just a girl.
Who slides closer so our bodies are touching.
I think to myself, 'could it be there?
In the dying horizon.
Hiding half out of sight.'

"How did we get here?"

...and here we are. Lightyears from a home we are supposedly defending. Lying in wait, spinning in the orbit of the distant 5th planet of the war zone star system. We know they're coming. We just don't know when. To sweep us away.

--

At the beach we gather with our offerings in hand. We release the sacred leaves that this morning the women and the children collected. We watch the leaves roll downstream like fearless pioneers. My daughter, a curious girl, looks instead upstream, ignoring the ritual.

--

Dazed. Fuzzy. The smell of food and the sound of speechless activity. I'm in a diner but I'm not hungry. The other patrons peek their wide eyes over their shoulders. The same look I imagine I am giving. There is a man sitting in the booth across from me who I have never met. He leans cautiously over the table and, whispering, asks me the exact same thing I am thinking. 'How did we get here?'

"Worst Case Scenario"

The worst case scenario. The missing piece. Heavy machinery with a singular purpose. The search for the black box. The missing piece. A bolt. A turbine. They hit the ground then the rest fall down. All the kings horses and all the kings men bend over and sift through the wreckage. Walking on egg shells.

--

There is no explaining what happens when you die. But we can explain how it happened. We can try. It doesn't answer the question we really want to know. But it answers the question we can answer. It won't be easy. It won't be enough. But it'll be something. The way they search for that black box, the missing piece, you'd think they were digging for salvation.

"Ashlands"

The Ashlands are coated in the dusty broken promises of the Ashman. Simon says put your hands on your head. Put your hands on your head. He taps his cigarette and opens his mouth to speak. "Simon says spin in a circle--

Keep spinning in a circle til Simon says stop."

Rock breaks scissors, scissors cut paper, paper covers rock. But the ash gets into everything. And the Ashman is waiting. Waiting for you to slip. Fleeting little whirlwinds kick up and burn out giving the Ashlands some kind of likeness of being alive. But the Ashlands are not living. "Stop spinning--

Why'd you stop? Simon didn't say stop spinning."

"Syzygy"

At syzygy, once a generation. Ancestors past and future, gather 'round the Stonehenge. When we talk we do not use language. Because it so often changes. Sharing the many meaningless details of our worlds wouldn't do anybody use. Conversely, there is no expiration on wisdom, or those human truths. And we only have so much time together.

The sky turns purple and the children play under the moon. They've no distinction of what is within or beyond the natural world, weaving between the enduring stones. Warrior chiefs painted blue, a long faced distant race with glowing cufflinks, laugh as the children weave between them too.

"Desire Path"

Desire path is a road where nobody put a road. Formed not by design but by necessity.
It could be a shortcut from one place to another. Or that piece of land that says no trespassing but people nonetheless traverse.

That no man's land between backyards. Where street cats sometimes give birth. With little cracks in the fence slats where you can see into other peoples kitchens and bathrooms.
That overgrown patch of grass which continues on where the sidewalk leaves off. Worn down into a thin strip of dirt which keeps on going.

Behind that service road where the trucks beep as they go backwards. Driving over transmission fluid and piss, mixing them into a primordial soup outside the loading dock of CVS.

The fallen tree and stones to cross the creek, littered with used matches and condom wrappers. Broken branches and smashed wild flowers lead to the abandoned silo where me and my first girlfriend first made love. We didn't plan to it just happened.

Stuff all felt different on the way back, took on an unfamiliar significance, holding hands more firmly, returning down that same desire path we climbed to get there.

WHISPERS

Children in the streets whackin' the cement with some sticks they found. Over and over. Hittin' the ground. One of them got an eyepatch. No doubt one of those sticks doin. When I listen I detect a certain musicality to it. A high pitch drum. But which perhaps threatens something awful to come. And one of them stops hitting his stick and looks right up at me here. And the stick in his hand is no longer a stick. It's become a spear.

~~~

I met with a man today who lived in what is now the former Yugoslavia. I asked him, 'what is it like to come from a land which now no longer exists?' He paused for a while. He looked me up and down and in my eyes as if I were his brother; and in a heavy accent answered me with his own question, 'Have you not heard of Eden?'

~~~

There's a reason you can't see my hands. It's because I want it that way. If some things touch you they can leave a mark and some of those marks don't wash away. One thing I will say, shakin' hands with a man you don't know, you're taking a chance. I got the hands of a man who's too trusting. Some men got hands which fold out into blades.

Grandpa left us a picture of himself as a young man. In it, he is standing beside the one our family calls 'strange smiling man'. In the background is a map of indeterminate geography. 'Where is this place?' we wondered. 'Who is this man?' and of course we all asked, 'Why does it appear as if grandpa is holding by its hair a severed human head?'

~~~

The dancing half-man half-boar is practicing in the forest. He asks himself at the end of each set, as he dabs the sweat off his pig nose and straightens the fur on his neck, if he is now good enough for the city to accept him.

~~~

We don't need cops here. We got the rocks. We make our votes with a good hard throw. Words don't weigh down the scales of justice like stone.

~~~

We had an enemy once. And we conquered them. And took their land because we liked it more than our own. And took their food and ate like them. And took their clothes and dressed like them. And took their gods and prayed to them. And took their women and had children with them. And steadily. And suddenly. We could not tell ourselves from them.
~~~

Its in the tones of whispers. Its in the banjos and the guitars. Murder ain't something what just goes away. Even when folks ain't speakin' it, they're still speakin' it. Secrets is something what sticks in the throat, even if any us don't know what the secret is. Police hot in their whodunit tasted sweet tea made like this before. It elicits a tisk of the tongue. A slight 'n unsettlin' sour.

~~~

Repairs in the shade. Sweat from the day cooling on my skin. Race went well even if we didn't win. Reflecting on lessons at my own pace. Smoothing over scrapes doing repairs in the shade.

~~~

Last night I saw a forest. And in that forest was a fallen bridge. And by that fallen bridge were a family of dogs. The father dog started pushing his pups into the chasm that the bridge once spanned. Couldn't say why. The dog didn't seem to know why either. But he kept pushing one pup after the other closer and closer to the edge until it fell. When the mother saw this she immediately ran toward her mate and threw him from the cliff, by instinct. He fell sickeningly into the rubble and the brush. For a while the mother dog sat with a sad far off look in her eyes while the remaining pups play-fought at her feet.

I remember on the radio hearing a piece I've never been able to find since. It was a chaotic screaming of instruments, sundry, unharmonious and ugly to the ear, but increasingly corralled by the drums which hit so authoritatively. It was strong. Unusual. And haunting. Evocative of a dark encroaching sludge. When it was over the DJ did not mention the band who composed it, but did say that the song was called, 'The Unification of Germany'.

~~~

The dogs biting at himself again. But hes not itchin'. The kids checked his fur and it ain't fleas. What pains this dog is grief. His love, a bitch, got hit by a car last week. He was the one who saw it. He came barkin' at us, tryin his best to let us know what happened. We walked out maybe thinking it was a squirrel. Kids came out too. We're talking to them about death, danger, sadness and whatnot. Poor dog though, these are human emotions its feeling. And hes got no way of dealing with them.

~~~

One man flew above the sleepy town in his nightgown. Surprised, feeling lively, and unwilling to come down. Why deny the magic the night has gifted him? In the morning was spotted by one or two early risers. Singled out as an abnormality by the punctilious sun. The flying man crash-landed quite violently behind the rationally drawn borders of the National Forest.

I mean, there's *the* Mount Everest but we got a mount 'everest' too. There's always a riot in one city or another. There's always a war somewhere in the world. Also there's boy here who done himself in. Out by the school he used to go to. He liked to rile himself up about them riots and wars but didn't get much of anyone to listen. Our 'everest' is green with a slope-slide hill you can walk up and roll down. Got a picnic area at the top.

~~~

We got a group together and set out to warn people of the mob that has come to terrorize our town. A frightened old woman opened her door and when we informed her, she gasped, 'Oh my, I was told you were them!'

~~~

Last night, a strange thing happened at the ballet. A man dressed as some sort of black creature entered the stage. He wasn't dancing. He wasn't gesturing. Only blindly running in zig zags between the dancers, limping and screaming along the way. My wife, an avid follower of the arts, was sitting beside me so I asked her, 'Is this part of the performance?' She leaned in and said plainly, 'Depends on the day. On some times it is. And on some times it ain't.'

I live in a world filled with explosives
Where everything is blown out of proportion
The people are giants
Because they never stop growing
And they die
Once their eyes are blind to the rest of the world below them

~~~

Pretty girls. Drivin' round in broke down cars. Lookin for the right guy for to fix it up for 'em. She'll watch him pop the hood with her tongue in her teeth and he'll drive away with her number. 'Give me a call when you think of a way I can repay you', she recites. And that's how love works in this town. Works every time.

~~~

We had a wonderful smoke in the stairwell, this strange woman and me. We had to be quiet as to not wake the agents in the adjacent rooms. We were not allowed to be there. And smoking no less. But we silently lit up and exchanged nods and a conversation worth of expressions and gestures. When she finished her cigarette, she left. And although I didn't even know that woman's name, I understood something deep within her. What that was precisely, I am not sure I can, or ever will, be able to say in words. Words are too heavy a tool, you see. I watched the smoke from her last breath hold in the air and it kept me company.

SLAM

"Perfect Words"

you know what to say
in these situations
with no explanations
oh just the right thing to say
just what you thought about
with logic and reason
and did the unthinkable
then what did you say?
oh just the right thing
something profound and reflective
something everyone can make sense of
but its only just a fancy way to fall

you let me know you left me
with a kiss and a gift that was small
enough to say you care
but you don't love me
it was kind but perfunctory
your lips were a cold stonewall
and the music was sad enough
with that one note of hope left
and you picked it so perfectly
to harmonize with the occasion
leaving me grieving
so poetically i almost forgot
it was happening to me at all

i don't have words for these feelings
that you pull so freely
and deal in ideally
to comfort those you wish
to kick around like a ball
now tell me the words

that you wish to part with
that you know i'll relive
that last precious moment
i'll keep like a photograph
that will poignantly linger
you know that i'll recall
replaying in my head
starting when your footsteps
echo into silence down the hall
will those perfect words make up for it all?
will they make up for it all?

"White Flowers"

send me a letter
where ever you now are
from a magnolia
white flowers
soft as skin

tell me the story
if you still remember
how it was we met
'neath white flowers
soft as skin

i only see them
as if they always are
when they're bloomin'
with white flowers
soft as skin

why cant i help
succumbing to the year
folded in your arms
white flowers
soft as skin

"Blockchain YHWH"

Blockchain YHWH. Beat inflation. Fleets of VOC* carry a country's GDP in the form of leaves and peppercorn. The mermaid whore sells herself by the sea shore. And sailor men spend a years worth of work for ten minutes with her. Gold and other alchemical substances. I stole to buy more holy medieval indulgences. They cut up Croesus and split him up into a million pieces. Lydian priests don't give out blessings for free. Your soul is nothing but another currency. I hope I don't die at a bad rate of exchange. But its like Brennus explained, before throwing his sword on the scales in his favor, 'Woe be to the vanquished.'

*Verenigde Oostindische Compagnie (Dutch East India Company)

"Twin Tricks"

Twin tricks splitting sticks and twigs indistinctly mixing pixies Dutch and Dixie fixing doppelgänger reindeer games tracing waning phases through the gates of Canaan blaming neighbors framing men who look the same as you.

Gotta lot of schadenfreude caught aboard a yacht about a stowaway to walk the plank not allowed to plead his case when arrived a giant tidal wave eradicating all those waiting bated breath mouths agape sea salt tasting crew.

The reach of the leash between species decreases each distinguishing breech frequently seizing another reason to research the first Neanderthal realizing every step of the way that we all share the very same shoe.

"Copper Island"

A coup on copper island flew in from forgotten Zion. The past crow has his considering eyes on the shimmering shores hes set his spies on. These unsuspecting highborns hoisted on petards shaped like electrical pylons. Picturing how they'll settle the score with talons invincibly gripping what they hang their power lines on, this city doesn't know what it has store. They don't remember the birds from before and the war of folklore set in this foretold December. The famous wren and the revenge of Saint Stephen. Even when its this close to the end these people don't seem to see them. Leave it to the kingdom to release a carrier pigeon with a message never again to be read by anyone. It's terrific to see the children of the Chalcolithic grow up to be women and men but they spent their last penny on an eagle who won't ever come to their defense.

"Dolphins"

we saw dolphins
on a cloudy day
the air was cold
the sand was wet
its not that beach
we remembered to going

the rain was mist
which came and went
the windshield wipers
might dryly screech
until you or i realized
where our minds were roaming

the view was bleak
our shoes were muddy
the seaweed scattered
from higher tides
not much to do
not much to see
neither of us knew
marine biology
do we hold hands
like this was the past
we both ask ourselves

“i don't know” i replied
when she did speak
a question so callous:
“why did we come here?”

but i did know
when she first arrived
i could almost hear seagulls
i thought she heard them too
unless i was mistaken

walking too long
not wanting to sit
not wanting to stay
not wanting a wasted trip
tired but still trying
pale and dreary and arid
any artist would give up
painting a picture of this

“dolphins!” she exalted
“i saw them too!”
another one sprung up
and another
each one incredible
both of us wept
holding each other to the grey sky
fins splashing and spinning
where the sun, could we see it,
would have set

"Beginnings"

The beginnings of things. The morning bells ring. A stray glance drawn by chance at an introductory meeting. The beginnings of things, when you're trembling and it's exciting that you don't know anything. The beginnings of things, thrown into a scene. The characters are new and slate is clean. The way it should be. The cries of a baby are music to me. Beginnings are the best part of a movie. Rewind and rewinding. Don't show a second of the middle or ending. The beginnings of things, stores may as well close after the grand opening. It'll never better than than it was at the beginning.

"Anubis"

Dropped hard on the lockbox, they chop up the unknown until its overt. Insinuations in the Swiss Guard take charge with every hit of the halberd.

--

I seen seventeen Byzantine Jesus statues gesturing blessings all in a row. But damn that was a while ago.

--

Sebastian ain't lying, but you gotta find him and that cracker jack magnifying glass can't catch a Spanish outcast.

--

Detective Greg tells his family he chews bubble gum to keep from smoking. 'Don't you knock' he hollers waving the air around his mouth.

--

Tainted smoke bellows from the very bowels of the Vatican on the pope's inauguration. Celebration is marred by a furtive odor. It's them burning the archives again.

--

Meanwhile Anubis slicks his ears back, fixes his headdress and gets to work.

"A Moment of Silence"

after the last plane jet
and last car engine
and the last foot step
and the last bug buzz
and the last bird chirp
and the wind dies down
and the dust dissipates
and the desert freezes
into a snapshot
in one brief flash
like a jackpot
like a revelation
like an island
there it arrives
a moment of silence

A NOTE ON BEAVERS

I have become aware of a certain revealing feature of the beaver. A small, seemingly irrational predilection that pushes him to perform his signature function. He has an innate extreme nagging dislike for the sound of running water. Primarily what drives the fabled architect to build his wooden dam is to quell that irritation. Displeased with the imperfect habitat he finds himself, the beaver sets out make his own improvements—to silence the interminable babbling.

It is from those peculiar motivations that entire ecosystems, little worlds, are created from out of no more than branches and a stream. The bugs and the fish and the birds who benefit from the beavers hard work all have that aspect of his grouchy nature to thank.

CLASSICAL

A NOTE FROM THE AUTHOR: I entreat you please, to not read the following pages in silence. Say them (Sing them!) out loud to yourself or together with others. Even better, dispense with the book entirely and put them to memory. This next section is meant to listened to.

"Cultural Anthropology"

Cultural anthropology.
The kids all come to watch me.
Pa says not to cross that bridge.
That's where the wild beasts live.

I think I seen them wandering.
Hair on their faces hiding where smiles might have been.
Fatter than they want to be and makeup masking their rougher skin.
Devotion and jealousy. Regret and anguish.
These are the trading cards the wild beasts play with.

Pa says not to cross that bridge.
Where all through the night loud music plays.
And they hold each other in exquisite ways.
Wherever they go bottled up barley follows.
Drawn to walk to where they'll be hurt the most.
There's something there that I have to know.

Pa says not to cross that bridge.
Please Pa don't be disappointed.

"Savior"

Gas stains and holes.
Yeah those are all new ones.
Two days by road.
These clothes in ruins.
Can't catch a tow engine blown in a Jericho heat.
Blisters have grown and then bursted now bleed.

Rocks in my shoes.
Rubs a soothing massage.
Laces come loose—
Ant'delluvian knots.
But I'm not gonna stop til this odyssey ends.
Because savages crawl 'ere they're civilized men.

Filthy and sore.
All the more like a martyr.
Become a new form.
Not of mortal but harder.
When underworlds start to feel something familiar.
Salvation resembles an eighteen wheeler.

Scratched up knuckles.
With mud on his face.
Seatbelt unbuckled.
By broken e-brake.
A trucker on speed handing over a J.
Is what looks like a savior on a day like today.

"The Portal"

When the magic is right.
A portal appears.
With a freedom one night.
Unfelt for years.

A bridge which exists.
That is mostly unknown.
Covered undisturbed.
Inches deep in the snow.

Archaeologists.
May dig with a shovel.
But the past is more fragile.
Than leather or bone.

Thickets and branches.
Partition the path.
The outside world.
Fractured; detached.

The lamplight emits.
From a five point star.
The bridge it sits.
Atop an ocean of tar.

A sphinx and a snowman.
Play practical jokes.
Try to get you to join in.
But you call them a hoax.

Remember that girl.
When you tried to show her.
But then the trail ended.
The fantasy was over.

Now you're alone.
Supernaturally cold.
Leaving your tracks.
In the cotton white snow.

When you meet toe to toe.
A familiar set.
By a break in the bushes.
And a teen silhouette.

Companion emotions.
Nostalgia; regret.
Walk side by side.
Reunited old friends.

"First Turnout"

The first turnout.
Where the particulars of the city you left are minuscule but not out of sight.
The words of goodbye and the pangs of regret still echo.
The mountain is high and you've only taken but one step away from a past life.
Standing lightly but defenseless bereft of all you'll let go.

There's roadsigns for rockslides and snowstorms ahead but you packed spare tires and chains.
You haven't yet decided if this is your forward charge or a coward's escape.
In this middle place.
Between somewhere old and somewhere new.
The first turnout sure displays a formidable view.

"The Golden Horn"

The golden horn.
All things orange. Was love ever so simple?
—
In Constantinople you're bound to run into someone you know.
Fastidious record-keepers require us unscrupulous folk to gain entry via alias.
Dispatches and plans are for honest Anatolians; while we villains must happen by chance.
—
I've lost a lot of loves to the Bosphorus.
Her disappearing mists hit most thick in the dawn.
You can sit and watch the ships for hours.
This one bears colorful wears from Ashkelon.
Offloading fresh fruit and disembarking strangers.
There's always another boat coming.
And any one she may be on...

"The Battle of Bull Run"

Lyin' on Manassas
The battle's almost done
The skeeters and the grasses
Backlit by the sun
Made a pillow from my packs
And set aside my gun

Left my home and family
Against their fulminations
Before that taste of glory
Reaches expirations
Proudly part of history
Marchin' on with Lincoln

Dead injured or dyin'
Can't no more than sit
There's only so much time
To make the most of it
Philosophizing dandelions
Floatin' thoughts Potomac

I wonder if my children
Will visit where I've lain
In case I ain't with ‘em
By subsequent campaign
This life is a vacation
Almost like a game

Drums and bugles buzz
The dead they all get up
Collect their replicas
Period--‘sixty one
Plaques say "Park Closed at Dusk"
"Here WAS The Battle of Bull Run"

"Camping in the Basement"

Camping in the basement.
Where I almost never go.
It's hard to face the darkness.
In the meditative cold.

I'm gonna spend the night.
Away from those I love.
To listen to their footsteps.
Rumbling above.

Camping in the basement.
Beside the shaky shelves.
Which hold the ornaments.
Of our forgotten selves.

I will sleep on concrete.
So they can sleep on down.
To sacrifice a keep.
To secure a royal crown.

Camping in the basement.
Like a king in his dungeon.
What could he be thinking?
To lock himself within?

Surpluses piled up.
In the torch's narrow glow.
He knows if there's a need.
He can always go below.

Camping in the basement.
Comforted by the depths.
Fortitude secures.
And prison walls protects.

The night is gothic silent.
But the kids are safe in bed.
I'm alright with nightmares.
If they can dream instead.

"Undeniable"

Ice melts from the sidewalks.
Color returns to the sky.
Mouths of the liars are silenced.
Replaced by songbirds of July.
Irrationality overextends.
The rickety bridge collapses.
The text it can be read in full.
Despite their mandatory classes.
Notes compared.
Why were we there?
Only because we were told.
I ain't waiting.
For an explanation.
Behold!
Beauty is undeniable.

"Chuck Heston"

The monkey make up wears off.
As seen through the nets and the bars of a cage.
The prison walls all plaster from brownish grey quick-drying paint.
Naked before an orangutan jury--That arrogant class of ape!

Chuck Heston sipping a whiskey after a long day at Fox.
Practicing lines and laughing to himself.
From his home overlooking the studio lots.
A simian view of the Los Angeles Basin.
Which first took shape in the upper Cretaceous.
Tomorrow's location, the Jurassic rock of Malibu.
“What life once existed beyond those ridges?"
Charlton mutters to his empty tumbler,
"Huh, haha, why couldn't it come true?”

"Gold Miners"

One way relationships. Sunburnt streets.
She left lonely wet footsteps coming back from the beach.

Faded flags hang in sedated blues and reds.
There's a sunset where dreams and the ocean intersect.

Love lasts a moment and it glimmers off the coast.
LA holds the gold miners who ran out of west to go.

"Artificial Moons"

Artificial moons lookin down at me with dead eyes.
Pumped full of electricity to appear like they're alive.
Artificial moons givin' me the creeps.
They've been showin' sooner since these winter weeks.
Streets with no sidewalks. And houses with no doors.
Neighborhoods with no people. And cities without stores.
What are they for?
Artificial moons blink on in the twilight.
And cast unnatural shadows all through the unnatural night.

"Arts District"

Palm tree paintbrushes wave their bristles.
Bent to the pencil grip of an unseen creator.
Who generously dabs orange from his pallet.
There's a magic here at the arts district.

The FAA say helicopters gotta stay low.
You can't pay for more powerful drums.
So I hum along to the sirens and alarms.
There's a magic here at the arts district.

Shattered glass mosaics on the pavement.
In the shadow of a tower eclipsing the sun.
Got my car broke into but I can't stay mad.
There's a magic here at the arts district.

"Mist on the Sacramento River"

Mist on the Sacramento river.
I can almost see Bartle's bridge.
Decisions and I don't make a quiver.
Not a breeze or the flopping of a fish.

Sycamores and willows straddle the county line.
Shedding seeds and dangling their branches.
Only lonely oaks on the other side.
Could acorns be a sign of second chances?

Squirrels bicker o'er the last remnants of the winter.
A car drives by on some unseen road.
There were fires on the hills, I remember.
Mist just resembles a better smelling smoke.

Stars shone clearer than ever last night.
The dusk was crisp and new and clean.
Can I trust them crepuscular insights?
Lying paralyzed in between a dream.

The fog clears up as the dawn breaks noon.
Power lines and buildings join the forest.
Squirrels hide as the bridge comes into view.
Then the wind causes my fishing boat to twist.

"William Blake"

I wanna meet angels
Like William Blake
To taste what he tasted
Drip walls away
Erase the rectangles
Watch views dissipate
The clouds and the bushes
Amalgamate
There you can see them
Where the edges fade
Break into the kingdom
Float over the gate
To the moon coliseum
Where phases await
A stone's-throw to meet them
My senses astray
I'm falling I'm falling
Into the paint
I'm falling I'm falling
Into the paint

"The Arrow"

Gravity seemed to suspend in that crucial micro second
When an era came to an end in a manner aptly trenchant
How vicissitudes can bend as an archer will his weapon;
Letting loose a most transformative missile.

The aide spake facetious in the outbreak of conflict
On steep Peloponnese cliffs exhibiting an Athenian gauntlet
Confusing canting with serious speech instead of being taunted;
Ignoring the Aegean winds inauspicious whistle.

Empty Quivers send shivers down the spines of physicists;
Glimmering fission blizzards pioneer a brand new neolithic;
An arrow aviates after it is delivered, rectifies and then hits;
Leaving behind no earthly or divine acquittal.

"Ganymede"

Cast your rocks on your own conscience.
Astrology and tea leaves have lost their speech.
Bipartisan oracles staunchly on the fence.
PREVARICATING on their high mountain peaks.

Feet on the ground and heads in the clouds.
They don't want to take sides in conflicts like these.
Aphorisms and riddles haven't helped us by now.
Just ask CROESUS how he values their vague prophesies.

A HERMIT engineered a flying contraption.
Deriving inspiration by his genius alone.
A testament to mankind's aptitude for invention.
Vexing those gods so high on their throne.

For they have abducted our beloved Ganymede.
Snatched for his beauty by Zeus from his flocks.
Disguised as an eagle but revealed as a thief.
I implore you RIGHTEOUSLY cast your rocks!

Vote white or black stone when the census is taken.
The black stone a surrender to the lurid divine.
White to save Ganymede from the constellations.
Riding a winged chariot of our own design.

"A Fine Place to Fall in Love"

Hopping the crosses of the train tracks.
Watching the horses gallop in the paddock;
Nudging each other with their noses.

The distant lake makes waves only if you're still enough to listen.
The traffic whooshes over bridges where lovers can be hidden.
Over rocky beaches that may be empty save disinterested fishers.
Convoluted trails and lonesome hikers in need of kismet.
Foxes share scraps from quickly cleaned up picnics.
Decorative flowers grow bouquets just waiting to be picked.
And the sun comes out only long enough for boy and girl to kiss.

Alas the chimney's of childhood beckon yonder lovers home.
Letting go until tomorrow of her soft and slender hold.
Bittersweet at dinnertime smelling pine with windows open.
Transfixed by the blanket bed of needles and ripening of cones.
Or wondering if she too is missing him every bit as smitten.

Quite out of the blue the young man proclaims to an audience of none,
"Today every living thing became just a bit more than it was."
His mother smiles at her husband,
He knows why, because
This sure is a fine place to fall in love.

"The Bachelor"

Escaping from the island of Circe
—The Bachelor absconds!
After half a season of reality TV
—suffocated by blondes.

Repulsed by the smell of roses
—snapping to his senses.
In a last ditch midnight jailbreak
—he's jumping the fences.

Tiptoeing past a plaster statue of Cupid
—'neath the security cameras.
Edging around the heart shaped pool
—'twixt Scylla and Charybdis.

Ornate mosaics on the floor of the seaside villa
—with an ocean view.
Mostly obscured by T-shaped tape marks
—and a production crew.

Was he naive to look in this place for a soulmate?
—let alone find her?
She, voted away as part of the game
—America's say in the episode decider.

If you thought you found your Penelope
—inside of a tacky romance.
Would you wait around for a fake finale?
—or would you take your chance?

"Land of Knives"

From their sabertooth tiger deity.
To their barbaric marriage rites.
And vials of blood used for money;
Nice guys don't survive in the land of knives.

The trees all have gashes celebrating.
Carved young lovers initials intwined.
Valentines day here means lacerating.
The native acacias and the pines.

They don't eat meat with a fork or spoon.
Who proudly display their family crest.
Hormones presage Fall's blood moon.
The season when love is in its harvest.

That beautiful girl who two young men wish to wed
She'll watch them dance first between themselves--
The deadly duet.

A NOTE ON STONES AND POEMS

A good poem is like a stone—substantial, defined, indifferent to its changing environment. Some stones have stood in one spot for millennia, obstinately out of place, displaying the enduring grandeur of it's own incomparable creation.

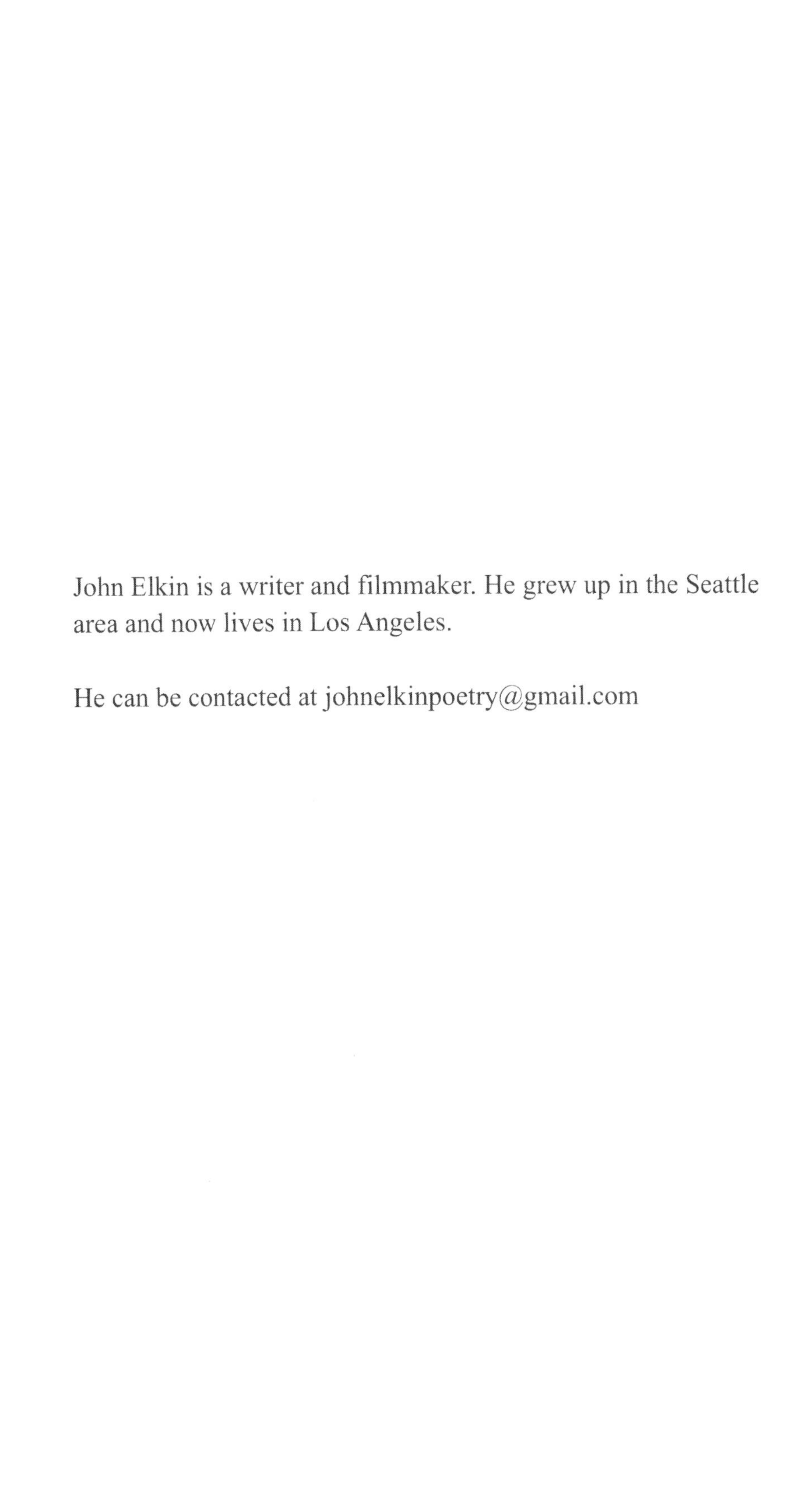

John Elkin is a writer and filmmaker. He grew up in the Seattle area and now lives in Los Angeles.

He can be contacted at johnelkinpoetry@gmail.com

Made in the USA
Middletown, DE
02 December 2022